A MOTHER'S PEN

by Margaret Hall

Carol,
May this book encourage you,
comfort you and/or inspire you.
Enjoy! Peggy
Happy Birthday!!

ISBN 978-1-63525-124-1 (Paperback)
ISBN 978-1-63525-123-4 (Digital)

Copyright © 2016 by Margaret Hall
All rights reserved. No part of this publication may be reproduced, distributed, or transmitted in any form or by any means, including photocopying, recording, or other electronic or mechanical methods without the prior written permission of the publisher. For permission requests, solicit the publisher via the address below.

Christian Faith Publishing, Inc.
296 Chestnut Street
Meadville, PA 16335
www.christianfaithpublishing.com

Printed in the United States of America

This book is dedicated to my loving husband and soul mate, Louis; my inspiring son, Scott; my precious and beautiful daughter, Laurie; my three loving stepsons, Tony, Terry, and Louie; my many precious grandchildren and great-grandchildren; and to the memory of my dear, dear mother, Georgiana. Thank you all for the love, patience, and encouragement through the years.

To the memory of my mother, Georgiana Elizabeth (James) Budde (October 11, 1916–May 24, 1965) for her love of poetry, her faith and the inspiration she instilled in each of her nine children; and to my youngest sister, Betty, for all the love and encouragement she has given to me.

To God be the Glory!

When you get married
and live on a hill,
send me a kiss
by the Whippoorwill
by Georgiana James
"George"
Birthday October 11, 1916
139 North Center St.
Plainfield, IN
"Your Sister"

Foreword

This collection of poems and prayers
represent a lifetime of a mother's
trials, tribulations, heartaches, joys,
celebrations, and love for her family.
May it help, encourage, and lift the heart of every reader.

Whatever you ask in prayer, you will receive, if you have faith.

—Matthew 21:22

Trust in the Lord with all your heart and lean not on your own understanding.

—Proverbs 3:5

Preface

My parents, by the Grace of God, brought
me to the Lord as an infant
in Holy Baptism and continued to raise me
in God's Word, allowing the Holy
Spirit to strengthen my faith the foundation of my writings.

Being raised in a family of nine children—
six boys, three girls—afforded
me the perfect opportunity to explore
poetry. We were always making up
rhymes just to pass the time, or to tease
one other. You know, like "Ray's
a baby, I don't mean maybe. He cries all day just to get his way!"

I wrote a lot of poetry as a student, but
never kept it. However, as I was
raising my family, I used my poetry as a
form of release and prayer to cope
with all the difficulties in life—unemployment,
dealing with a "blended"
family, sickness, rebellious teenagers and
young adults, and to express many
of the joys in my life. I also used poetry in
my church life as a witness to
others or as a persuasive tool. This is a
collection of all that poetry blended
with poetry by my children and grandchildren, and used with their
permission.

My Mother

Her eyes were brown,
Her hair was black
But streaked with silver gray.
Her smile was soft,
Her temper rough;
But I loved her anyway.
She had a sense for knowing
Just what was going on
Inside my head,
Inside my heart;
My love for her was strong.
When I was sad, she understood
And always knew what to do.
When I was glad, she'd smile at me
And tell me she was happy too.
Then in the spring of sixty-five,
God chose to take her away.
He took her home to live with Him
On that twenty-fourth day in May.
Now she's not sad and not in pain
From that awful cancer anymore;
And I'll be glad when I can greet my mother
On that beautiful Heavenly shore.

A letter written to my eleven-year-old son after he'd gone to live with his father.

To my dear son whom I dearly love,
You were a gift from God above.
I held you tightly to my breast
And vowed to love you 'til my final rest.
And as the years have been and gone,
You've brought me joy as naught has done.
Oh yes, the tears have been there too,
But that's all part of raising you.
And now, my son, we're far apart
But you'll always be there in my heart.
Besides! My son, you're not just mine,
You are God's and He is thine!
He will guide you in your ways
So give Him thanks and give Him praise.
This is just your mother's little verse
To tell you things aren't so bad…
They could be worse.
If you are happy, then I am too
Because, my son, I truly love you!

Mother

Lou

There is a man, his name is Lou.
His hair is brown, his eyes are blue.
He is not short, he's five eleven;
When he kisses me, I'm in seventh heaven.
And when he tells me, "I love you,"
I'm glad he's mine—this man named Lou.
He gives me love so sweet and kind;
He's got his faults but I don't mind.
I've got just as many as he, I'm sure.
For that, my friend, there is no cure.
It matters not, for we know who
Gave His life for me and Lou.
He died for all, Our Savior dear
He died for all, without one tear.
And since His love is dear and true,
We give our thanks, me and Lou.

Terry and Deb

Although they're young, they're much in love.
Their eyes shine bright like stars above.
They've gone through hell to get this done—
In just three days they'll be as one.
For better or worse, they'll go through life;

MARGARET HALL

He'll be her husband—she'll be his wife.
And so our prayer for them will be
That they'll love each other,
Eternally!

Count Your Blessings

As I sit here pondering about my life,
I find that among the pains, heartaches, and strife…
I've been so richly blessed by God!

My faith, of course, is number ONE;
Called by the Holy Spirit and purchased by God's own Son.
I've been so richly blessed by God!

A loving husband tops my list of blessings.
Then comes five children, three made mine
through love and caressings.
I've been so richly blessed by God!

And, oh, the grandbabies!—seven now and two on the way.
Their precious existence brightens each day.
I've been so richly blessed by God!

It's funny how the pains, heartaches, and strife
Just seem to disappear from amidst my life
When I count my blessings from God!

Seek and You Will Find

Seek Him in the morning
And ask the Lord to stay.
He'll be more than happy
To guide you through the day.

Seek Him at the noontime,
Reflect on morning past.
Then go about your business
With a peace that's sure to last.

Seek Him in the evening,
Ask Him to forgive.
And thank Him for the blessings
That He was glad to give.

Seek Him last at bedtime,
Ask for a restful sleep.
Tell Him that you love Him.
Your soul He's glad to keep.

Seek the Lord everyday
And you'll begin find
A blessed reassurance
And a constant peace of mind.

The Broken Heart

Silent tears roll down my cheeks
As a few days seem like weeks.
Even though time seems to fly,
The hours pass slowly by and by.
No one can know—no one can see.
Only God knows what tortures me.
Not even I, the one who hurts so much,
Knows why I cry at a loved one's touch.
Could it be I'm just growing old?
Or is it that this world is cold?
Is it that I miss my son?
Or has the change-of-life begun?
For the answers, where do I go?
And do I really want to know?
I just want the pain to cease.
I need some rest and quiet peace.

This was written to encourage and read to any ladies in our church whose husbands had been laid off from work during a big labor dispute.

The Lord works in mysterious ways
His wonders to perform.
He brings proud people to their knees
Amidst a terrible storm.

A first reaction at lay-off time
Is—"How will we manage now?"
Believe me, friend, as time goes on
The Lord will show you how.

He'll humble your heart and bend your knee
And teach you how to pray.
He'll give you strength and build your faith
And see you through each day.

So cast your cares on Him, my friend;
He truly cares for you.
I speak from many months of learning —
The "crunch" has hurt us too!

A MOTHER'S PEN

Oh, Holy Spirit, enter in
Within my heart, Thy work begin.
Create a faith so strong and true
That I shall ne'er depart from You.

Count me among the Heavenly Host
Praising Father, Son, and Holy Ghost.
And while I'm here on earth today
Let my faith so shine in every way

That some poor soul may see Your light
That brightens a day or dreary night.
Oh, Holy Spirit, enter in
And in my heart, Thy work begin.

Spring's flowers bloom
Summer's sun beats down
Fall's leaves start fading
Winter's snow comes down.

From sight to touch
To smell, to sound
That's the way God
Made the world go 'round!

MARGARET HALL

"Thy will be done," is easy to say
But accepting it—another story.
I'd rather think that I know best
Instead of giving You the glory.

But I soon find out, I'm not as smart
As I'd like to think I am.
You teach me quickly that
You're the Shepherd
And I'm the little lamb!

My heart is heavy, my nerves are frayed.
My temper's short from a worried mind.
Oh, God in Heaven, how I've prayed
Knowing that You will be kind
And give me rest from my fears.
Tell my troubled mind "Be still";
And when I shed unwanted tears,
Remind me, Lord, it is Thy will
For him to be so far from me.
I trust that he is in Your care.
Keep him always close to Thee.
Oh, Heavenly Father, hear this prayer!
I've kept silent, oh so long
Kept inside, the things I feel
I'm so weak, but You are strong
Help me Lord, so I don't steal
Precious moments from those at home.

Our Daughter

The thunderstorms came and went
Into the world a girl was sent.
Her eyes were blue, her hair was brown
She turned our lives upside down.
Her little cheeks were rosy red
Her nose turned up just like a sled
Her fingers and her toes were right
Her body sweet, we held her tight.
Yes, this little girl is our queen
And we named her Laurie Eileen.

The following was sent to my daughter while she was in Naval Boot Camp:

Once you were a baby
With blue eyes and a curl
Then you grew to become
A sweet little girl.
Soon you were a teenager
And all hell broke loose—
Sometimes I thought
Your neck fit a noose!
But now you're a woman
God knows I'm so proud
That often I walk
With my head in a cloud!
You've got what it takes

MARGARET HALL

Just let it grow
And soon you'll enjoy
The navy, I know!
She became an aircraft mechanic in the Navy and loved it.

Dear Louie,

Someday you'll find this and then you'll see
Just how much you really mean to me.

When you're in pain, I hurt too.
When you're upset my life is blue.

When you are happy, I'm all aglow.
You see, my sweet, I love you so!

When you're bewildered, I'm confused.
When you feel silly, I'm amused.

When you feel "frisky," I'm ready dear.
As long as we live, I'll be here.

So, my darling, I love you so,
Through rain or shine or winter snow.

You're my life, my breath, my all
'Til death us do part, we'll have a ball!

Love you forever,
Peg

Give Me Strength

As I grow older and wiser—I hope,
I see the strength You give me to cope.
Not just yesterday or the day before,
But now and always—forevermore!

I see the need to search Your Word
And find Your peace—Oh, help me, Lord.
For all too often I'm lax to follow
The wisdom You give—then I feel hollow.

So, give me strength just one more day.
In Jesus' name I humbly pray,
Amen.

Lord God,

    Our Heavenly Father, if Thou see fit to someday make us wealthy on this earth, Let this our prayer be—
That we should have the kindest heart, help those in need with all humility.

    But if Thou see fit to keep us poor, may we live with hope and love and thankful hearts for the riches we now acclaim.

You sent Your Son -He died for us; in this
we are rich -we have eternal life with you.
Oh God, we praise Your name,
Amen.

My God, How Great Thou Art

When I wake in the morning,
And see the sun start to rise
Yet, find the moon still peeking
Between the clouds in the skies;
When I feel the breeze hit me
In the face and blow my hair
And see the leaves falling
Like feathers through the air;
When I hear the birds singing
And the traffic buzzing by
Or hear the mailman greet me
With a friendly little "hi";
When I see a neighbor helping
Another to rake the leaves
Or watch an old man shooing
The pigeons from the eaves;
When I can see the beauty
That surrounds me from the start
Then I'm compelled to say—
My God, how great Thou art!

A MOTHER'S PEN

Luck

They say a million dollars will make your cares go 'way
But give your cares to Jesus when your bow your head to pray.

A pinch of salt is worthless—so is a penny in your shoe.
Your only "luck" is Jesus—He died to save you, too.

There's all kinds of sayings to help you in your strife;
But there's none true 'cept Jesus;
He gives Eternal LIFE!

Dear Father in Heaven,

I come to you in great sorrow for my sins, forgive me. Thank You for sending Jesus to suffer and die for me that I might have forgiveness that I don't deserve. Thank You for loving me. Please help me to love You more.

    I have a great desire to be a good and faithful Christian, but it is so hard and I'm so glad that You are so gracious and forgiving, and have promised to hear my pleas.

    Father, I've been so depressed about so many things; so depressed that I've fallen into Satan's temptations of self-pity, neglect of trusting You. Anger, yes, even thoughts of suicide. Oh, Father, forgive me!

    Send Your Holy Spirit to strengthen me. I'm so weary.

    Lord, I'm so thankful for my husband's unemployment because You've taught me how to fully depend on You, but it's also getting to me. Please strengthen me and help me to bear this cross for Jesus' sake.

    I ask that if it is Thy will, please help him find employment or to be called back soon to his former employment. And, Lord, please help me to accept Your will.

    Father, if it is Thy will that he goes back to work soon, keep us in check that we don't get too proud and neglect you again. Help us to give back to you a fair share of what you've given us.

Help us to serve You gladly and willingly and faithfully.

Father, as You have forgiven us, give us forgiving hearts that we can forgive our enemies as Jesus did on the cross. Help us to love all people, but especially our fellow Christians.

Help us to discover the talents that You've given us so that we can use them to serve You and glorify Your name.

Father, teach us to pray without ceasing, to live with an attitude of prayer, and to teach our children how to pray.

Father, be with our Pastor and help him to be a good and faithful Shepherd to his flock which You have given to him.

Heal the sick according to Your will. Bring the lost sheep back to the fold, and have mercy on me and all repentant sinners.

In Jesus' name, I pray,
Amen.

My Dearest Kindest Friend

It never fails, that when I need Him most,
My precious loving Savior is such a gracious host.
He attends my every need and then takes special care
To tenderly reassure me that He'll always be right there.
He never ever asks me, "Could you make it NEXT weekend?"
His loving arms are always open—He's my dearest kindest Friend.
He never tires of listening to my troubles or my tears
And He always knows the perfect way to calm my many fears.
He never bids me go, instead He asks me to stay
And only wants me to love Him, trust Him, and pray.
So, when all seems lost and life is hard to bear,
I know my precious loving Savior will always be there.

A MOTHER'S PEN

How Blessed Am I?

My heart cries out in despair
For those who know not "hope";
For the many souls in this world
Who know not how to cope.

My heart cries desperate tears
For the minds who know not "peace";
For the tired and crippled bodies
And the hunger that does not cease.

My heart cries in desperation
For the souls in Satan's snare;
For the children of this world
Who only live to know despair.

How blessed am I to know Your love
And the peace of mind You give.
Help me share these precious gifts
With the world in which I live.

When you're feeling very lonely, turn to God for He is there.
Keep Him in your heart forever; always talk to Him in prayer.
Ask Him always to forgive you, for we always need His care.
We are His for now and ever, He will answer all our prayer.

Oh, for a verse to sing Your praise
Or a song to sing my thanks
For all Your answers to my prayers
And Your peace within my soul.

Oh, for someone to hug
And tell them of Your grace;
Or a child to hold and love
And whisper Jesus name into their ear
To tell them of our Heavenly goal.

Tender Shepherd

Once upon a time, there walked upon this land
A very tender Shepherd and He was oh, so grand!

When e'er His lambs would stray, whether young or very old,
He knew just where to find them—His love was pure as gold!

He never failed to watch His flock by day or by night.
No matter what the danger was, they relied on His great might!

This very tender Shepherd offered up a sacrifice
To save His flock of sheep, His own life was the price!

Jesus is the Shepherd and we are His sheep.
He still watches over us, for Jesus does not sleep!

Father,

Thank You for this day now ending
With rising moon and setting sun.
And may my Shepherd ever tending
To His flock, keep me as one

A MOTHER'S PEN

Of His lambs, so helpless still,
Safe through this night
All according to Thy will.
Amen.

The words won't come,
Oh, pooh!
I wanted to write a poem
And write it just for you.

But as I sit and ponder,
Oh, fiddle!
My thoughts go to and fro
And all I've got's a riddle!

The following was written and read to encourage and invite more women to participate in the work of our Lord…

The Ladies Missionary League
Extends their WELCOME to you.
Please join our Christian fellowship
And see just what we do.

The Ladies Missionary League
Is work and also fun.
We laugh, we sing and with God's help
We try to get things done.

The Ladies Missionary League
Offer you their greeting
So serve the Lord with gladness
And come to our next meeting.

MARGARET HALL

See you there in September!

Dear sisters in Christ, let's be reminded
That the tongue can be a dangerous thing.
Let's not use it to demean another,
Let's use it to praises sing.

If we don't carefully choose our words,
Or the tone with which we speak,
We could cause a sister's faith
To go from strong to weak!

Where are You, God?

How long will You stay away?
My patience grows thin
As I continue to pray and pray!
That's it! Teach me to be patient
As I long for You to hear
And give me an answer
That'll help me cope with what I fear.
I know You're not gone,
That You're with me here and now,
But it seems that there's no answer
To my pleas of "tell me how!"
Tell me how to manage
On just my salary alone.
Tell me how to smile
As I work my fingers to the bone!
Tell me how to be patient
When the bills keep coming in.
Tell me – how do we go on
And face it with a grin?!
Tell me how, Lord,
As I read Your precious Word,
To know that You still love me
And my prayers have all been heard.
Oh, Father, please forgive me
For questioning Your ways
And help me learn to give You
All my thanks and praise!
Lord, thank you for my husband,
And the children whom we share.
And thank you for my job,
I know You really care

Behind a Prison Wall

Behind the prison wall, the Gospel MUST be shared
For Jesus said, "Go into all the world"—He knew, He cared!
But, murders, thieves, and robbers?! You say?
Oh, my dear Christian friends! Get on your knees and pray!
For each time you've hated someone or sat down on the job
You're as guilty as those who openly steal and rob!
Yes, you and I are no better than they;
But by His loving Grace, He showed us the way
And commands us to go and share His Word
With all of His lambs who have never heard
And with those who have heard but gone astray.
Let's share God's Love, let's teach them to pray.
I'm by no means saying they should not serve time,
But God offers forgiveness for even their crime.
Christ died for all—not just you and I;
He died for sinners—even those sentenced to die!
Now, not all of us possess the talent it takes
To go into a prison -for there, Satan awaits!
But each of us does have the talent to pray
For those who are gifted in that special way.
Jesus said, "I was in prison and you came to Me."
Oh, what does it take for us to see
That He wants us to go behind prison walls
To teach His Truth, to heed His calls?
I know what it takes—I was blinded once, too
But God opened my eyes, now He wants me to help you.

You see, one of your Christian brothers is there;
And this is something that's hard for me to share.

A MOTHER'S PEN

He's my son—a Christian boy who went astray
And I've learned so much in the year he's been away.
He got in the wrong crowd, drinking, drugs—the whole bit.
So I asked God to jerk his head around if He saw fit.
"I don't care how, just do it," I said.
He did! But not at all in the way I'd thought in my head.
But God's ways are not ours I quickly was taught;
For armed robbery of $32.00—my son was caught!
My son?! With his Christian upbringing?
"You self-righteous sinner," God said. And my ears kept on ringing.

Then I remembered I'd said I didn't care how
But, oh Precious Jesus, what do I do now?
"Cast all your cares upon Me," I read.
"I will deliver you and you will glorify Me," He said.
God answered my prayer —He'd answered my plea
And then through my son, He comforted me.
"I was going astray, Mom. God knew just what to do
To bring me back to Him—and to you."

So, Christian friends, that's what it took for me to see
The great need there is for "prison ministry."
Behind the walls of prison, there is a lot of fear
And many hearts and souls are open just waiting to hear
The Gospel news of Jesus and how He died for all,
His offer of forgiveness—even behind a prison wall.

In God's Loving Grace,
A Christian Mother

My son was eighteen years old at the time and served six years in prison. He now has a family and is doing well. He loves Jesus and has a heart of gold. I am very thankful that God kept him safe in prison and brought him back to teach others from his experience.

Following are some poems he wrote during his incarceration—used with his permission.

> I walk down a corridor and what do I see?
> Lonely faces staring back at me.
> He'd like to think he's different, but he never can.
> I'm just an ordinary man.
> Can he make some changes? Should we lend a helping hand?
> It's time to see the faces; it's time to ride the land.
> Play me some mellow music and let me reminisce
> I'll look outside the window—how those years I miss!
> Let me shut out the world and dream
> And face it the best I can.
> I'm just another ordinary man.

Trust God

> Lord, help my unbelief and doubting;
> Turn them to trust and confidence.
> Let my heart and soul be yours
> That my faith requires no evidence.
>
> Turn my desire for revenge
> Into helping that lost soul.
> Rearrange my thoughts, Lord
> That doing Your will is my goal.
>
> Open my heart to be forgiving
> When my enemies cause me pain.
> Teach me that through Your grace
> I've Eternal Life to gain.

Mystical Amusement

The truth is hard to come by; it hides behind a veil
Like the wind upon the ocean might hide behind a sail.
Curiosity of our world is forever in our reach;
Yet it sucks away faith, like blood, as if a thirsty leech.
It twists us to its pathway and makes you want to turn.
It says, "You are the student, and this you'll want to learn."
Mystery and Magic, is this, that which you crave?
Well, here's the spade and shovel, boy. Go ahead and dig your grave.
Don't ask it any questions and it won't tell you any lies;
For this will open up your eyes, and you will surely die!
Just one way to come above this—take up the path of the Lord;
For you are saved through Jesus and He'll take up your sword.
Some things weren't meant to know, some things just to test;
And believe the Lord, Son of God, will put you at your best.
So remember this when you begin to meddle
with things you misunderstand—
If what you ask was meant to know, God would put it in your hand.

About the effects of Dungeons and Dragons (the game)

MARGARET HALL

Written during the turmoil of waiting for my son's trial…

Wait

Let me see the sunshine
Amidst this stormy sea;
Let me hear the calm
Among the waves that torture me.
The ship is slowly sinking
As the storm continues on;
I hear Your voice but faintly
And I'm barely hanging on.

Oh God, You are my lifeboat.
Please come and rescue me.
The storm is raging fierce;
I'm drowning in this sea!
Oh, let me see the sunshine,
Let me know Your peace.
Let these clouds pass over
And bring a gentle breeze.

Only You can save me
From the perils of this storm.
Only You can change the cold
Into sunshine, sweet, and warm.
Oh, hear my SOS, Lord,
That I'm sending urgently;
Calm this storm, send Your peace—
I wait, Oh Lord, on Thee!

This poem was written in the spring of 1990 while my husband was home recovering from a quadruple bypass. It was inspired by the view from our kitchen window.

Beware

The little Robin just sits there
On the fence—so unaware
Of all the danger that surrounds him
Fly away little Robin—Beware!

His song is sweet, his manner calm;
He's looking for some food to fare.
Yet all around him, danger lurks!
Fly away little Robin—Beware!

He jumps down to get a worm;
He hasn't got a prayer!
The cat is crouching, ready to pounce.
Fly away little Robin—Beware!

Well, what do you know! He flew in time
And escaped his foe with ease.
Come back little Robin
And sing to me—please!

Father, I know not what to do,
So in this prayer, I come to You.
You see Lord, I am so down hearted
My brother and his wife have parted.
People say 'tis not my affair.
Should I speak out? Or do I dare?
Tell me, Father, what to say.

MARGARET HALL

Guide my words in such a way
To help them see the things they've done
And to come to know Your Son.
For Lord, I fear they have forsaken
You, Your Word—they're so mistaken!
You've promised that You'll answer me
As I pray unceasingly.
So, dear Lord, I ask this favor—
Help them to know and love their Savior.
Use me, oh God, if it's Thy will.
I'll do my best to fit the bill.
He's my brother, she's his wife.
Help them Lord, to live this life
With love for You within their heart—
It isn't good that they should part.
But Heavenly Father, You know best.
Please give my heart a little rest.
I love You —I love them too.
Oh, tell me, Lord, just what to do!

When you're weak and feeling lonely
Turn to God for He is there
Keep Him in your heart forever
Always talk to Him in prayer.
Ask Him always to forgive you
As we always need His care.
We are His for now and ever
He will answer all our prayer.

There's dusting and sweeping and mopping to do;
And laundry and dishes and such.
There's ironing and mending and groceries to buy
And, oh my, the work is so much.
Now the pay leaves a lot to be desired,

A MOTHER'S PEN

But I've benefits by the score
'Cause all of this work is meaningless
'Cept for the family I do it for.
This family has a special place
Within my heart, you see.
'Cause this family isn't just a job—
This family belongs to me!
We're not always together though,
Sometimes we're far apart;
But only in miles and distance, 'cause
We're always together in my heart!

"Franny," the fashion bug—
So cute and so funny.
She must have a room for her shoes;
How about for her "Money"?

Oh, my goodness! This girl's got class!
She dresses in style
Each day of the year,
Not just for a little while!

She flits from "here" to "there"
So fast I get dizzy!
And that's a real jolt for me,
Her "old" friend, Lizzy!

I'd considered another topic
For this little diddy, my dear—
You know—your gorgeous outfit
With your YELLOW ring in your ear!

Written for a co-worker, Sunshine, on July 26, 2007, during my lunch hour.

Count Your Blessings

Have you ever tried counting your blessings
When you thought that you had none?
Well, why don't you start with, "I woke up today
With the rising of the morning sun?"
Then after your first cup of coffee
And when you think you're able,
Count the food you've just prepared
As you're setting it on the table.
Next, as you hear your children complain—
"Not this again, Mother, oh dear!"
Don't forget to count as a blessing, too.
Each voice that you can hear.
I could go on and on I suppose,
But I hope I've made it plain
The next time you think you've no blessings to count,
Just stop and think again!

Praise God from whom all blessings flow!
And help me, Lord, to always show
Just how thankful I truly am
For saving me, Your little lamb!

May we our jobs do well for Thee
And seize every opportunity
To give You thanks and give You praise
And show Your love in ALL our ways,
Amen.

A MOTHER'S PEN

The sun's gone down and darkness draws near,
As I come to You, Lord, I know that you'll hear
My deepest thoughts, my silent tear.

My thoughts and prayers are for those I love.
My tears are joy and thanks for Your grace from above.

And in the midst of my prayer and song
I ask You to help me love those who've done me wrong.

Be with those who are alone; give comfort to those who have grief.
And with the love that You have shown,
I ask that those in pain might have relief

Lord, thank You for being in my heart—
Thank You for loving me from the start.
Amen.

A Mother's Springtime Prayer

Oh, Heavenly Father, be with me this spring.
I'm counting on help with everything.
From making beds to planting seeds;
From washing walls to hoeing weeds.
The windows need washed; the screens need sprayed;
The curtains need mended—the hems are frayed.
Closets need cleaned and there'll be canning to do—
I'm counting, Dear Lord, on help from You.
But above all, don't let me stray—
Nor fail to thank You for each day.
Remind me often that You care,

MARGARET HALL

And help me, Lord, Your love to share.
Use my talents what e're they be
To thank and praise and glorify Thee!
Amen.

A Birthday Poem for Our Son-in-Law, Steven.

Dear Steven—We just want to wish you
a very Happy 39th Birthday!
We hope you know we love you
And perhaps you wonder why.
Well, let's just stop and ponder
As we breathe a long deep sigh—
It could be that you're married
To our daughter, don't you see?
But no, that's not the reason
So, just what could it be?
It could be your good looks,
That runs in our family—
But no, that's not the reason—
So what else could it be?
It could be that you're a musician,
We're music lovers don't you know?
But no, that's not the reason
Or we'd have told you long ago.
The reason we love you, Steven,
Is two-fold and very true.
You are a child of God
And you show it to be true!
We love you, son,
Ma and Pa Hall

How dead in its faith this church would be
If our only task was to worship Thee
Instead of arming ourselves with The Holy Spirit

A MOTHER'S PEN

To take the Good News and joyfully share it.
What good is faith if works are not there?
And what good are works if our heart doesn't care?

Every Christmas at my place of employment, we have a Christmas potluck. Employees invite their spouses/significant others and it is a large feast. Needless to say, the refrigerator in the breakroom must be cleaned out, in order to accommodate the many dishes needing to be kept cold until lunch time. One December, a cashier and I volunteered to come in on a Saturday and clean the fridge. It was a chore that we did not anticipate… it hadn't been cleaned like we cleaned it for a very long time… hence, I decided to write a little poem, have it laminated and attached it to the front of the refrigerator with magnets. This is what it said:

Step right up and open my door.
I'm here to provide a place to store
Your lunch, or snack, or your favorite drink.
But, please keep me clean so I won't stink.

I may be a "fridge," but I'm just like you.
I like to be clean and fresh smelling too.
So when your belongings are one week old,
Remove them from me before they grow mold.

Your thoughtful efforts will help me feel good
Because I'll be able to work as I should.
So don't be thoughtless, stubborn, or mean…
Just kindly help to keep me CLEAN!

When I retired, I brought it home for my own "fridge!"

Thank you, Lord, for this day
Come in and be with me today.
Give me strength to do my chores
Give me time to be out doors.
When my children need me most,

Help me be a pleasant host.
Keep me from the devil's wiles,
Fill my heart with loving smiles.
When my husband comes home tonight,
Help me be a welcomed sight.
You have blessed me with Your love
And with Your Spirit from above.
If it's Thy will, when this day's done,
Let me awake to greet the sun.
Thank you, Lord for this day.
Come be with me, show me the way.

Kitchen Closed

The kitchen's closed due to illness
I'm "sick" of cookin' meals.
I'd sooner go to the show
Or read Seuss' "Bears on Wheels!"

The kitchen's closed due to illness
I'm "sick" of cookin" food.
I've washed the clothes, cleaned the house;
I'm just not in the mood!

The kitchen's closed due to illness
I'm "sick" of figurin' out
What this one likes or that one hates
I'm ready to scream and shout!

The kitchen's closed due to illness
I'm "sick" of feelin' this way
I'd just love to go out and eat
After all, it's Mother's Day!!

Lord, as I rest my weary head
And think of where my feet have tread,
I pray that every place I've been
I'll have the chance to go again.
For, as You know, and I know too,
My witness has been lax for You.
If You should give me one more day,
I ask that You will guide my way.
Give me the words to speak Your truth
To rich, to poor, to old and youth.
I'm just a mother, wife and such
And I depend on You so much
That I oft forget You count on me
To spread the news that sets us free.

Forgive me, Lord.

The Wayward Christian

There's a song in my heart, but it's hiding
There's a smile on my lips, but it's suppressed.
There are words in my mind, but they're not forthcoming.
There's a deep longing to speak within my troubled breast.

Then I asked You to help me as I searched among Your truths.
"Ye have but to ask and it shall be given;
Seek and ye shall find;
Knock and the door will be opened."
And Your Spirit took hold of my mind.

Now my heart is singing
And my lips smile with glee.
The words are now forthcoming.
Lord, I'm glad I came to Thee!

When I was president of our women's group at our church, there was much dissention during the meetings due to other groups within the church taking on tasks that had once been done by our group; hence, this poem was born:

A Prayer of Concern

Dear Lord,
How awful it must be for new members coming in,
To sit through a meeting where dissention reigns within.

As we grow in number, there's bound to be some change;
But surely not our Christian love do we want to rearrange!

The officers do their best with what they've been taught;
And yet the atmosphere is not what it had ought.

It should make no difference which "group" we happen to be.
We all should work together to win lost souls for Thee.

Lord, forgive the bickering and all the silly fuss;
Forgive the snide remarks among the group of us.

Help the new ones learn and the older ones to teach;
But only in a Christian way, for the lost we want to reach.

Give us peace and understanding and Your forgiving love;
And may we always praise Your name on earth and heaven above.

In Jesus' name, Amen.

We've all been the recipients of Divine Grace
and we have the obligation to
share it. Let us be about the Lord's business in love and harmony!

The following two writings were written by my daughter as we waited in the ICU waiting room, after a quadruple bypass on my husband/her dad was done—May 4, 1990. She asked that I include this in my collections—.

When a loved one is at risk, our minds wonder and we think of many "what ifs?" We go from chair-to-chair; to the cafeteria, the payphone; wherever we think we can pass more time. We hear machines beep and then we take a deep breath. Then the phone rings and we wonder what the news is that we'll hear. These things make us wonder and we need our Friend.

Our Friend is our Savior, Jesus Christ. Without Him, we couldn't make it through the "what ifs," the passing of time, the beeps, and the telephone rings. He brings us comfort, love, truth, courage, strength; and He gives us Himself. He's watching over us all at all times.

The surgery went well because our Friend was guiding the doctors' hands and was keeping Dad strong. The recovery is going well and Dad knows that his Lord is on his side. Things will work out for the best with everything in God's hands.

Thank you, Jesus, for being our FRIEND.

MARGARET HALL

Waiting

Waiting again ... that's what I'm doing now.
Mom's asleep, but I'm not tired somehow.

Here we are in this waiting room, passing time again.
But what do I write with this paper and pen?

My heart is full of joy for Dad's doing so well.
Without you Lord, to pieces I would have fell.

I look at Dad and I look to the skies.
I thank you so much, tears fall from my eyes.

I'm lucky I have you, my Savior, my Friend.
And I entrust to You my Dad—my other friend.

by:
Laurie Hall

Laurie

Laurie, Laurie, quite so fair
Where'd you get your pretty hair?

Laurie, Laurie, ever true.
Where'd you get your eyes of blue?

Laurie, Laurie, oh so sweet,
Where'd you get your giant feet?

A MOTHER'S PEN

Laurie, Laurie, you're so cute;
You'll grow up to be a beaut'!

Written when Laurie, our daughter was a tiny infant.

To our youngest son, while he was incarcerated…

A letter a day
Keeps my blues away.
A letter a week
Keeps me at my peak.
A letter a month
Is better than none.
But not at all
Makes me BAWL!!
Start writing!

Written April 4, 1986

In case you ever wonder

Let me reassure your heart
Of all the love I carry…
Very deep within my heart.
Even in the bad times…

You mean so much to me.
Oh, son, I truly mean it.
Understand and believe!

MARGARET HALL

We Have Roots!

We've got a tree in our backyard, it's not good for much at all
Except causing lots of trouble in the Spring and in the Fall.
The trouble stinks! I mean it smells! —and not of any flower.
It never fails, it always happens when I am in the shower.
This tree has roots—I don't mean "kin."
They grow over hill and over dale and through our pipes again!

An invitation sent to family members to
attend Christmas dinner at our
House—we had a wonderful turn-out!

Once a year's just not enough
For a family to gather 'round and stuff.
But even so, on Christmas Day,
Perhaps we all can make our way
To join in PEACE and HOPE and LOVE
And share these gifts from above.
It is the season to be jolly
With mistletoe and Christmas holly.
We'll share good food and have some fun,
But we won't eat 'til after one.
So make your plans, be on your way
For a very SPECIAL Christmas Day.

See you at our house!

Jesus blessed us all when He sent Susanna here.
She's so sweet and tender and such a little dear!
But now she has an "owie" and we know what to do.
We'll say a prayer to Jesus—He'll be her help, 'tis true.

A MOTHER'S PEN

Written for our Pastor's little baby who was
in a brace to straighten her legs.
(I was babysitting for them)

My daughter had a friend down the street from us who was moving away. It was sad for her and she wanted to give her friend something as a going away gift. She chose to give her one of her stuffed animals (Baby Beans, later to become "Beanie Babies"). I wrote the following poem to go with it…

Here's a gift to help you remember,
A girl who is glad to have known.
You and the rest of your family,
And all the love that you have shown.

So, when you pet "Lickety Leopard"
Someday when you're lonesome or blue,
Remember the girl who sent him with you,
And say a little prayer for her too.

This poem was written as a card to accompany
a baby shower gift (a baby monitor)
for our niece, October 23, 1993

The gift inside this box, though not one of a kind;
Serves an important purpose—Mommy's peace of mind.

Every tiny whimper, the softest little cry
That unexpected laughter will never pass you by.

You won't have to wonder or run to and fro.
You'll hear the baby calling no matter where you go.

With love,
Uncle Louie and Aunt Peg

Heavenly Father, hear my prayer, this horrible pain is hard to bear.
As You sent Your Son for me, help me bear this pain for Thee.
In my suffering send Your love, hope and strength from above.
When I sit and ask You, "why?" Hoping that You'll let me die,
Remind me Lord, of Your Son and all the suffering He has done.
Amen.

The following was written twenty years after my mother passed away on May 24, 1965—two days before I graduated High School.

In Memory of Our Mother

The golden days of sunshine turned to rain that day,
When angels came down from heaven and took you home to stay.
Your suffering days were over that twenty-fourth day of May,
But we were left bewildered to face life's dreary way.

Now a score of years is past-we're still treading down life's road,
And you're still sadly missed by the young and by the old.
Farewell again, dear Mother, we shall weep no more,
For we plan to meet again on that beautiful Heavenly shore!

In loving memory of Georgiana E. Budde

A MOTHER'S PEN

Written for and sent January 16, 1993, to my oldest stepson while he was in prison...

> We have but to ask and He will keep us safe.
> We have but to ask and He will be our guide.
> We have but to ask and He will see us through.
> We have but to ask and He'll keep us satisfied.

Written for our daughter's friend when we were unable to attend her performance in the school play...

Dannell,

I know we said we'd be there, but things just didn't work out.
So don't go throwing a fit or crying, and don't you dare pout!

We've heard the play is great, and "Frenchy"—you've been a smash!
So keep up the great performance —the
house'll come down with a CRASH!

Good luck and break a leg!
Love,
Louie and Peg

Written to my brother-in-law when he was upset about being asked to contribute a large amount of money (at the time) toward a gift for his parents' fortieth anniversary...

So, you're past thirty, how about that?
You're still lookin' good —not even fat!
But, John, I'd like to say one thing, and it's the truth.
If you have love in your heart, you'll always have youth.

MARGARET HALL

    Quit worrying about the price you pay…
Mom and Dad may not always be there—someday.
    A fortieth anniversary is really quite nice
   And the memory of it all is worth any price!

         You'll see,
         Love, Peg

  A prayer for your recovery is on its way to God.
May He bless you, keep you and take away your pain.
     May He strengthen you, enrich you
     And put you on your feet again.

      Hope you're better soon!

A little "diddy" written and read to welcome all the ladies to our Zone Fall rally (our church was hosting the event and we served the noon meal), and I, as president of our group, was responsible for the welcome speech. I made it short and sweet.

    The ladies of Our Redeemer would like to
      welcome all of you here today—

        The soup's on cookin'
        The silverware's clean
      It's been fun and hard work
        Preparing this scene.

      So, with no further ado—
       We won't dilly dally.
       Just welcome you to
    The Decatur Zone Fall Rally.

A MOTHER'S PEN

I wrote quite a few poems to express concerns
about the happenings within
our ladies group at church. Following are some of them…

Dear sisters in Christ, let's be reminded,
That the tongue can be a dangerous thing.
Let's not use it to demean another,
Let's use it to our praises sing.

If we don't carefully choose our words,
Or the tone with which we speak,
We could cause a sister's faith,
To go from strong to weak!

Dear Friends,

Have you ever been asked to define a word? Many people have different meanings for that same word.

What is "Christianity?" I asked someone that question the other day and she answered, "Living a good life." Someone else said, "Christianity is belonging to and attending a church."

These things are a part of "Christianity," but just that—"a part of." I believe there is much more, such as faith in Jesus as our Savior and living that faith. It's also trying to live the way Jesus taught us—with love for one another, respect for one another, forgiving one another as our Lord forgives us. "Christianity" is also realizing that we are all sinners and that we don't deserve eternal life, but that our Lord and Savior, Jesus Christ, gave us eternal life when He suffered, died and rose again.

What do you think? What is "Christianity?"

Your friend in Christ,
Peggy

The following was written to encourage and invite more women to participate in the work of our Lord. Pastor included it in the Sunday Bulletin distributed at Church.

> The Lutheran Women's Missionary League
> Extends their WELCOME to you.
> Please join our Christian fellowship
> And see just what we do.
>
> The Lutheran Women's Missionary League
> Is work and also fun.
> We laugh, we sing, and with God's help
> We try to get things done.
>
> The Lutheran Women's Missionary League
> Offers you their greeting
> So serve the Lord with gladness
> And come to our next meeting.
>
> See you there in September!

The following was written and read to convince the ladies of our group that we needed to get involved with Prison ministry in some way...

On the last day, the ladies of Our Redeemer Lutheran Women's Missionary League stood before God's throne, and Jesus said unto them, "I was hungry and you fed Me." And they replied, "But we just gathered food for the needy and participated in the 'meals on wheels' program." But Jesus answered, "You did it for Me. Well done, good and faithful servants."

Then Jesus said unto them, "I was naked and you clothed Me." "But we just gathered sweaters and baby layettes for the unfortunate," they replied. Jesus answered them, "But you did it for Me."

Then Jesus said, "I was sick and you visited Me." "But we just helped purchase baby monitors for SIDS infants and we only sent cards, flowers, or mustard seeds to the ill." Jesus answered, "But you did it for Me."

Then Jesus looked at them and said, "When I was in prison, I sat in My cell and waited. I hoped and prayed for a letter, a visit, something to comfort me in My distress. I felt forsaken, unloved and alone. I was frightened—very frightened. I needed reassurance of God's forgiveness. I needed to know that I was not forgotten. Where were you? I needed you, but you weren't there."

The ladies looked astonished and said, "You mean You were in prison, Lord? We didn't know."

Jesus said, "Yes, I was there. There were many Christians in prison. Christians who went astray and had to pay for their mistakes. Christians whom I loved very much and needed to hear that, but no one was there to tell them or remind them. There were also people in prison who didn't know of Me or My love at all, but if someone would have taken the time to tell them, they could have had the chance to be saved, like you. Where were you when I was in My darkest hour? Where were you?"

We've been the recipients of Divine Grace, and we have the obligation to share it!

> Oh, praise the Lord for that great day
> When Pastor Cluver came our way.
> We prayed that God would bless our call
> And He indeed blessed one and all.
> We thank you, Lord, for this man.
> He teaches well, does what he can.
> He preaches truth and purity.
> For this we send our thanks to Thee.
> Lord, grant us still one more request
> That each of us shall do our best
> To listen well and follow true
> Thereby giving all glory to You.
> Amen.

MARGARET HALL

This was written for and given to Pastor and
Mrs. Cunningham, the day they
left for Marion, IA to pastor a new church.

Although our hearts are saddened
And our eyes so full of tears,
We know that God is with us
And He'll take away our fears.
You'll be missed upon your leaving.
We're sure you know we care.
And God would not have sent you
If He didn't want you there.
We thank Him for your guidance;
For your teaching of His Word;
For your caring, sharing, friendship,
And your faithfulness to the Lord.
We'll pray for those in Iowa
To be faithful, loyal, and true
To Jesus Christ their Savior
And of course, we'll pray for you.
So, God go with you to Marion
And keep you in His love.
We hope to see you again soon
If not here on earth, then in
Heaven above!

To a long lost nephew on his birthday—August 18

It's hard to express through laughter and tears
The joy of seeing you after all these years!
We'd learned to accept what we thought was our lot;
But believe me, Bryon, you were ne're forgot!
And now it's your birthday —what is it? Thirty-four?
May God bless you with many, many more.
And may He help us to keep in touch
Because, you see, we love you very, very much!!

A MOTHER'S PEN

HAPPY BIRTHDAY!

To a long lost great niece on her birthday... August 8
Brandy Michelle,
Today you're six and oh, so sweet—
From the top of your head right down to your feet!
So, don't you wiggle when pictures are taken
Or your cute little freckles will be blurred and shaken!
Have a very Happy Birthday, sweetheart!
We're so very glad to finally know you!
Love and hugs,
Great Uncle Louie, Great Aunt Peg
And cousin, Laurie.

To our long lost niece, Jan Marie (Brandy's mother)... she and her brother are my oldest brother's children whom we had not seen since his death in 1959. They were very young when my brother was killed in an auto accident.

So many years have passed
There's so many moments we've missed
But never a year went by
That you weren't mentally hugged and kissed.
You see, you were ne're forgotten
Our lives were just detained —
Only to be joyously re-united—
For our love has ere remained.

We were afraid we wouldn't know you
But much to our surprise
The Lord has well preserved them –
Your "princess" smile, his big brown eyes.
The joy within my heart
Just cannot be expressed.
I just know that I am happy

And feel truly, truly blessed.

We're SO glad to know you again!
God's blessings to you always.
Love, Aunt Peg.

To Bryon (long lost nephew), as he was heading out to sea again with his Naval crew... he had asked me to write him a poem to take with him...

Off To Sea Again

Do you know how hard it is to write upon demand?
So, these are thoughts of mine just written by my hand.

Well, it's off to sea again and this will go along
As will my love for you–my heart is full of song.

A song of praise and thanks for your presence in my life
For those four precious children and your special, lovely wife.

It's been so long since I've sat down to write.
I've been so busy from morning 'til night.
No time to rest, no time for fun.
It's rush, rush to go somewhere–for someone.
It's off to work and back home again—
Only to find more work to begin.
There's supper to fix and washing to do,
The tub needs cleaned and the groceries are few.
"I need this ironed," "I need this sewn."
Oh, how busy our lives have grown!

… A MOTHER'S PEN

A Baby Shower Gift Poem

Inside this package wrapped with care,
You'll not find a kitty or a teddy bear;
No hummingbird to sing a sweet song;
And no little bunny just hopping along.
The gift inside—neither fancy nor frilly
Will keep baby warm when the weather is chilly.

A Christmas poem for my nephew and family…

Just a note to tell you that we sure miss you so,
But hope this special season will set your hearts aglow.
We've been so darn busy, our letters have been few,
But that can never change the love we have for you.
I passed the term with A's, Uncle Louie's doing well,
Laurie's a legal sec'y; that's all the "news" to tell.
So, we wish a Merry Christmas to the Budde's on Key Street
May God keep us all safe until again we meet.
Love, Aunt Peg.

On the Birth of Another Nephew

Timothy Richard, your new little boy,
Shall surely bring you both much joy.
And as he quickly learns and grows,
He'll soon be stepping on your toes.
Then as the years come and depart,

You'll find him stepping on your heart.
Don't be discouraged, life's just this way.
So never, never cease to pray!
Teach him that he's God's own son—
That He loves us dearly one by one.
If you teach him this from the start,
He'll never really break your heart.
I'm sending this little poem to you
Because you see, I love you, too.
So give Timmy a kiss for me
And hug him oh, so tenderly.
May God fill your hearts with joy
And thanks and praise for your NEW LITTLE BOY!

Then I changed that one a bit, so I could send it for the birth of a new niece...

Wendy Marie, your new little girl
Shall surely set you both in a whirl.
And as she quickly learns and grows,
She'll soon be stepping on your toes.
But as the years come and depart,
You'll find her stepping on your heart.
Don't be discouraged, life's just this way.
So never, never cease to pray!
Teach her that she's God's own child
That He loves her dearly, sweet and mild.
If you teach her this from the start,
She'll never really break your heart.
I'm sending this little poem to you
Because you see, I love you, too.
So give Wendy a kiss for me
And hug her oh, so tenderly.
May God fill your hearts with bliss,
And thanks and praise for your NEW LITTLE MISS!

A MOTHER'S PEN

A birthday poem for yet another niece... on her first birthday:

Sara,

Happy Birthday, little one, even though it's late.
I even had it written down upon the proper date.
But as your Mom and Dad know well, and brother and sister too,
I'm terrible at sending cards, hope this rhyme will do.
A year ago on May fifteenth, God smiled and sent some love
He knew some folks who had a need for sunshine from above.
This gift God sent was wrapped in pink and
trimmed with a soft blonde curl.
And oh, the love flowed 'round this gift of a precious baby girl.
And ever since that day last year when God showed His love so true,
We've all been thankful for His gift—
His gift, sweetheart, was YOU!
Hope you had a happy birthday,
Love always, Aunt Peg.

Another birthday poem for a November day:

It's almost winter and yet not quite—
The temperature sometimes drops low at night.
Autumn's still here, winter's 'round the bend
But I have the warmest wishes to send.
I wish for you a "sunny" smile on a cold autumn day
And a "warm" tender heart as you go on your way.
But most of all, Elizabeth,
I wish you A HAPPY BIRTHDAY!

To my sister (I can't remember which one):

I don't know if this will be on time or if it'll be late.
But I just want you to know I think you're one of the great…
Sisters I have—though I only have two;
Friends I have—I don't have few;
Listeners I know—I don't know many;
People I know—you thought I didn't know any!
Have a Happy Birthday, sister of mine!
Love, Peg

A Birthday Poem for my Friend, Betty K

When God created the world, one of the
most precious things He made
Was a friendship like ours —a friendship that doesn't fade.
Too often, I forget to thank Him for a friend so dear to my heart.
But He knows how I feel about you, and has from the very start.
So, on your birthday, Betty, this poem is written for you
To wish you love and peace and joy and
thanks for being a friend so true!

Happy Birthday!
Love, Peg.

A Birthday Poem for my grandson, Phillip.

A little troll
Came out of his hole

A MOTHER'S PEN

Shouting…
"Didn't you hear?
Phillip's a year!"
And he scooted away to hide.
A little mouse
Came out of his house
Asking…
"Weren't you told?
Phil's a year old!"
And he hurried back inside.
A little bunny
All furry and funny
Whispered…
"Don't be waiting
Phillip's celebrating."
And he hopped away so fast.
A little squirrel
Scampering in a whirl
Stopped…
Looking real hard, he said,
"Send him a card!"
So, here it is at last!
Happy Birthday, Phillip!
Love, Grammy.

A get-well note to my daughter's sixth grade
teacher, Miss Sheryl Duff, at
the LSA:

Even though the weather
Is cloudy, cool, and "murky"
We're sure hoping you feel
Like being bright and "perky."

You're too nice a person
To be down with the flu.

MARGARET HALL

We like to see you smiling
And we like to smile back at you!

Get Well!

Written to a friend at Christmas time, 1993

Just a while ago we were strangers
But God caused our paths to meet.
He knew I needed a friend
So He sent me one so sweet.

Now, it's Christmas—
The time for peace, joy, and love.
A time for the giving of gifts,
And giving thanks to God above.

So, Heavenly Father,
Thank You for this friend you gave me.
Keep her always safe from harm.
Keep her heart filled with Your love.
Bless her smile and sweet charm…
Give her strength to face each day
And the trouble that may come
With courage and hope from You
Until her job is done.
In Jesus name, Amen.

Thank you, Edna
For sharing my laughter and tears.
For the encouraging words you spoke
When I told you of my fears.
This is not an expensive gift
But I know you won't care
'Cause it comes from my heart
And the friendship that we share.

A MOTHER'S PEN

A Blessed Christmas to you, dear friend.

Written to my stepson, but never mailed…

You know, we've made mistakes and we've butted in,
And we've spouted off—we're prone to sin … we're human.

We've butted in only because we love you.
We've spouted off only because we have feelings.
We've made mistakes only because … We're human.

What's happened to respect and love, and family ties?
They've turned into loathing, and hate, and ugly lies!

For months now, we've left you alone as
you both seem to have wished;
But the disrespect continues and the ugly lies persist.

And now it's close to Christmas—your message reached our ears.
But this game you play is harmful. It's caused us many tears.
And our hearts are getting hardened
This game's been played too many years!

You can kick a dog around and it will still be your friend.
But if you kick it once too often, it will die and that's the end.

This all started with "Cleo," a "type" of dog that I abhor
But I gave in as usual and came knocking at your door.

I gave in for your Father's sake and for your sister's too.
I thought we had a good visit.
Apparently, it wasn't good enough for you.

I could go on and on, but you know the game you've played.
I just wish you understood the terrible price you've paid!

MARGARET HALL

The damage this game has caused, will take a long time to repair.
We're willing to try—are you?
But only if you really care.

Dear Twila,

I <u>PLUM</u> forgot about today—
Being your birthday and all—
I'm so <u>BERRY</u> sorry!

I could <u>ORANGE</u> a little play
Or have someone tell a story.

But instead, I had a little hunch
Of a bowl of fruit with a little punch.

But I forgot the fruit—
'Cept in this verse.

And as for the play -forgot to rehearse.
So the story is in —I just told you one.

HAPPY BIRTHDAY, Miss FORTY-ONE!

Written for Twila by: Margaret "Peggy" Hall August 26, 2009

Merry Christmas to Millie, Mary Ann, Mary Anne, and Carolyn!

An autographed picture—just can't throw away;
That old '45 record—so long ago it played
The sock-hop, the lemonade stand
The pep rally, tryouts for band.

A MOTHER'S PEN

These are memories of long ago.

> The weekends come alive
> With friends, food and laughter
> Each Saturday night at five
> As we make memories to last hereafter.

These are memories I'll cherish forever.

> Each one of you has touched my heart,
> Prayed for me when things were tough.
> You welcomed me from the start—
> Been there through smooth and rough!

>> Friends like you are a blessing indeed.

>> May your Christmas be joyous and full of love.
>> Thank you for being my friends.
>> December 2009
>> With love,
>> Peggy

>> Friends are forever!

A 38th Anniversary (June 29, 2007) card for my sweet hubby:

Front of card:

> ***Few phrases in life bring me such complete joy as saying, "This is my husband, Louie."***
> ***Happy Anniversary, my darling!***

Inside of card:

I love you–You're my reason for waking, for smiling, for laughing,

sometimes for crying (when I fear losing
you). I thank God for joining
us together thirty-eight years ago.

I can't imagine life without you because you are indeed "the wind
beneath my wings." I would never have
gone to college except for your
encouragement, your confidence in me.

You are where I find my rest and comfort
after a grueling day at work.

When you hold me, or touch my hand,
or smile at me, I feel safe. I'm
comfortable anywhere as long as I'm with you.

I love how we so often (on a daily basis)
think and say the exact same
thing.

We are so much a part of each other that it is difficult to
know where you end, and I begin or where I end and you
begin. God said, "And the two shall become one flesh." I
know now that He wasn't just talking about sex, He was
describing the perfect relationship—our relationship.

Thank you for loving me for all these
many years and for your loyalty
and faithfulness.

I am so looking forward to the rest of our
life together—God willing,
we'll celebrate our 50th anniversary in 2019!

I love you so much!
Thanks for the gift of love.

When I told my fourteen year old granddaughter, Olivia, that I like to write poetry, she said that she also likes to write poems and sent me the following… she really surprised me with her PS! I asked her if I could include her poem in this book and she said she would be honored.

Nana you are so special
Your love knows no bounds
A room takes special warmth
Whenever you're around
You might think I'm cute and talented
And maybe even wise
But I know there's more to me
Through your loving eyes
Every day with you is precious
I'm so grateful for the time
Of all the grandmothers in the world
I'm thankful that you're mine.

P.S. I will never forget your smell.
Your smell is like your second signature.

—*Olivia*

Love Fulfilled

Two people fall in love, marry, hope, and dream of their future together—'til death they do part.

This couple is blessed with children, gifts of God, whom they love and cherish because they love and cherish each other.

They put their personal lives—each other—their personal dreams and aspirations on hold and concentrate on nurturing and providing for these lives entrusted to them. Helping each one to develop the wings of maturity needed to fly from the nest when the time comes. Doing the best they know how to provide guidance and trust. Loving each one as individuals, as each is unique.

Then the last child, the baby, grows up and flies out on her own. The parents, because they've had their lives on hold for so long, find it hard to let go. They've forgotten how to live for each other, forgotten how to hope and dream together about their lives. The child, because she's the last, the baby, spoiled, is afraid. She's afraid she'll fail, afraid to leave behind the security of the nest and venture into new and exciting worlds. Afraid that Mom and Dad do have a life without her.

Don't be afraid, my child. Spread your wings and fly! And don't look back—someday you, too, will have to help someone develop their wings.

Don't be afraid, lovers. The nest is empty only of children. It is still full of love and hopes and dreams waiting to be taken off the back burners. Let go of the children. God takes care of them now, as always. They are no longer children, but adults. Spend your time fulfilling your own dreams, loving and helping each other. June 4, 1993.

It took us a year to get over the "empty nest" syndrome. We now truly know what God meant when he said, "And the two shall become one flesh." He wasn't talking about just physical love...he was talking about emotional and eternal love.

We don't know where one ends and the other begins...we are one. We are Love Fulfilled. Praise the Lord!

About the Author

Margaret Hall was born in Plainfield, Indiana, on July 9, 1947. Her parents moved back to Illinois where she and her eight siblings were raised. She attended parochial grade school and graduated from Altamont Community High School in 1965, two days after the death of her mother. She contributes her love for poetry and writing to her mother's influence and encouragement.

After a young (just out of high school) failed marriage and birth of her son, she met the love of her life and her soul mate, Louis. They married in 1969. This blended family of his three sons and her son was blessed with the birth of their daughter in 1972.

Through trials and tribulations, this "match made in heaven and blessed by God" family was the instrument she needed to resume her writing—as a form of release. After all, raising a blended family of four boys and a daughter was no easy task. Thus, as a mother to five children and grandmother to nineteen grandchildren (lost track of the number of great-grandchildren), her love for writing flourished and produced *A Mother's Pen*.

CPSIA information can be obtained
at www.ICGtesting.com
Printed in the USA
FFOW03n0349280817
39333FF